W9-ASV-526

RED COPPER™ Skillet Cooking

Publications International, Ltd.

Congratulations and thank you for purchasing my Red Copper™ Cooking Cookbook.

If you are already cooking with Red Copper™, you know how easy it is to use and clean. You are going to love these new recipes and I'm sure many of them will end up in your weekly meal planning.

Make Mac & Cheese Bites for your next party or get-together, Easy Chicken Parmesan will take the family to Italy without leaving the house, and Pineapple Orange Snack Cake is oh-so-good and bakes right in the pan.

As always, don't hesitate to give the recipes your personal touch.

From my Red Copper™ Family to yours, Happy Cooking!

Cathy

TELEBrands PRESS

Telebrands Press
79 Two Bridges Road
Fairfield, NJ 07004
www.telebrands.com

Pictured on the front cover: Bacon-Crusted Hawaiian Pizza *(page 54)*.
Pictured on the back cover *(top to bottom):* Ham and Vegetable Omelet *(page 6)*, Veggie-Packed Spaghetti & Meatballs *(page 56)* and Emerald Isle Lamb Chops *(page 51)*.

ISBN: 978-0-9972597-5-9

Manufactured in China.

8 7 6 5 4 3 2 1

TABLE OF
Contents

BREAKFAST & BRUNCH

Cranberry Buttermilk Pancakes

1 cup all-purpose flour

1 cup whole wheat flour

2 teaspoons baking powder

1 teaspoon baking soda

½ teaspoon ground cinnamon

¼ teaspoon ground nutmeg

⅔ cup whole berry cranberry sauce, divided

2 eggs

2 tablespoons vegetable oil

1½ cups buttermilk

Maple syrup (optional)

1. Combine all-purpose flour, whole wheat flour, baking powder, baking soda, cinnamon and nutmeg in small bowl; mix well. Whisk cranberry sauce, eggs and oil in large bowl until well blended. Gradually stir in flour mixture until combined. Stir in buttermilk until smooth and well blended.

2. Heat Red Copper™ Pan over medium heat. Pour ¼ cupfuls of batter 2 inches apart into pan; cook 3 minutes or until lightly browned and edges begin to bubble. Turn over; cook 3 minutes or until lightly browned. Repeat with remaining batter. Serve with syrup, if desired.

MAKES 18 (3-INCH) PANCAKES

Ham and Vegetable Omelet

1 tablespoon vegetable oil

2 ounces (about ½ cup) diced ham

1 small onion, diced

½ medium green bell pepper, diced

½ medium red bell pepper, diced

2 cloves garlic, minced

6 eggs

⅛ teaspoon black pepper

½ cup (2 ounces) shredded Colby cheese, divided

1 medium tomato, chopped

Hot pepper sauce (optional)

1. Heat oil in large Red Copper™ Pan over medium-high heat. Add ham, onion, bell peppers and garlic; cook and stir 5 minutes or until vegetables are crisp-tender. Remove mixture to large bowl.

2. Return pan to medium-high heat. Pour eggs into pan; sprinkle with black pepper. Cook 2 minutes or until bottom is set, lifting edge of egg with spatula to allow uncooked portion to flow underneath. Reduce heat to medium-low; cover and cook 4 minutes or until top is set.

3. Gently slide omelet onto large serving plate; spoon ham mixture down center. Sprinkle with ¼ cup cheese. Carefully fold two sides of omelet over ham mixture; sprinkle with remaining ¼ cup cheese and tomato. Cut into four wedges; serve immediately with hot pepper sauce, if desired.

MAKES 4 SERVINGS

Egg in a Hole with a Hat

2 corn tortillas

1 tomato, diced

1 avocado, diced

¼ teaspoon salt

¼ teaspoon black pepper

¼ teaspoon ground cumin

Pinch ground red pepper

2 teaspoons olive oil

2 eggs

1. Cut round hole in center of tortillas using 3-inch cookie cutter. Combine tomato, avocado, salt, black pepper, cumin and ground red pepper in small bowl.

2. Heat Red Copper™ Pan over medium-low heat; brush with oil. Place tortillas in pan and break 1 egg into center of each hole. Cook 2 to 3 minutes or until whites have firmed. Carefully flip tortilla and egg; cook to desired doneness. Add cut out tortilla rounds to pan to warm.

3. Serve tortillas and eggs with tomato avocado mixture and top with tortilla round "hats."

MAKES 2 SERVINGS

Turkey Bacon Mini Wafflewiches

1 teaspoon Dijon mustard

1 teaspoon honey

8 frozen mini waffles (2 pieces, divided into individual waffles)

2 thin slices deli turkey, cut into thin strips

2 tablespoons cooked and crumbled bacon

4 teaspoons shredded Cheddar or mozzarella cheese

2 teaspoons butter

1. Combine mustard and honey in small bowl. Spread small amount of mustard mixture onto one side of 4 waffles. Top evenly with turkey and bacon; sprinkle with cheese. Top with 4 remaining waffles.

2. Heat butter in large Red Copper™ Pan over medium heat. Pressing with back of spatula, cook sandwiches 3 to 4 minutes per side or until cheese is melted and waffles are golden brown.

MAKES 2 SERVINGS

Fabulous Feta Frittata

8 eggs

¼ cup plain nonfat Greek yogurt

¼ cup chopped fresh basil

¼ teaspoon salt

¼ teaspoon black pepper

1 tablespoon olive oil or butter

1 package (4 ounces) crumbled feta cheese with basil, olives and sun-dried tomatoes *or* 1 cup crumbled plain feta cheese

¼ cup pine nuts (optional)

1. Preheat broiler. Beat eggs, yogurt, basil, salt and pepper in medium bowl.

2. Heat oil in large Red Copper™ Pan over medium heat, tilting pan to coat bottom and side. Pour egg mixture into pan; cover and cook 8 to 10 minutes or until eggs are set around edge (center will be wet).

3. Sprinkle feta and pine nuts, if desired, evenly over top. Transfer to broiler; broil 4 to 5 inches from heat source 2 minutes or until center is set and pine nuts are golden brown. Cut into wedges.

MAKES 4 SERVINGS

Tip: This frittata also makes a great meal. Cut it into quarters and serve it hot with fruit for breakfast, tuck a wedge into half a pita for lunch, or serve it alongside roasted red potatoes for dinner.

Strawberry Banana French Toast

1 cup sliced fresh strawberries (about 8 medium)

2 teaspoons sugar

2 eggs

½ cup milk

3 tablespoons all-purpose flour

1 teaspoon vanilla

⅛ teaspoon salt

1 tablespoon butter

4 slices (1 inch thick) egg bread or country bread

1 banana, cut into ¼-inch slices

Whipped cream and powdered sugar (optional)

Maple syrup

1. Combine strawberries and sugar in small bowl; toss to coat. Set aside while preparing French toast.

2. Whisk eggs, milk, flour, vanilla and salt in shallow bowl or pie plate until well blended. Melt ½ tablespoon butter in large Red Copper™ Pan over medium-high heat. Working with 2 slices at a time, dip bread into egg mixture, turning to coat completely; let excess drip off. Add to pan; cook 3 to 4 minutes per side or until golden brown. Repeat with remaining butter and bread slices.

3. Top each serving with strawberry mixture and banana slices. Garnish with whipped cream and powdered sugar; serve with maple syrup.

MAKES 2 SERVINGS

Sweet Potato and Turkey Sausage Hash

1 mild or hot turkey Italian sausage link (about 4 ounces)

1 tablespoon vegetable oil

1 small red onion, finely chopped

1 small red bell pepper, finely chopped

1 small sweet potato, peeled and cut into ½-inch cubes

¼ teaspoon salt (optional)

¼ teaspoon black pepper

⅛ teaspoon ground cumin

⅛ teaspoon chipotle chili powder

1. Remove sausage from casings; discard. Shape sausage into ½-inch balls. Heat oil in large Red Copper™ Pan over medium heat. Add sausage; cook and stir 3 to 5 minutes or until browned. Remove from pan; set aside.

2. Add onion, bell pepper, sweet potato, salt, if desired, black pepper, cumin and chili powder; cook and stir 5 to 8 minutes or until sweet potato is tender.

3. Stir in sausage; cook without stirring 5 minutes or until hash is lightly browned.

MAKES 2 SERVINGS

Sausage, Egg and Biscuit Bake

32 frozen potato nuggets

4 eggs, beaten

8 brown-and-serve sausage links, sliced into rounds

½ cup (2 ounces) shredded Cheddar cheese

9 refrigerated biscuits

1. Preheat oven to 400°F. Spread potato nuggets in bottom of Red Copper™ Square Dance Pan.

2. Add eggs and sausage; sprinkle with cheese.

3. Top with biscuits. Bake 10 to 12 minutes or until biscuits are brown and eggs are set. Remove from pan; cut into nine squares to serve.

MAKES 8 SERVINGS

Apple Monté Cristos

4 ounces Gouda cheese, shredded

1 ounce cream cheese, softened

2 teaspoons honey

½ teaspoon ground cinnamon

4 slices cinnamon raisin bread

1 small apple, cored and thinly sliced

¼ cup milk

1 egg, beaten

1 tablespoon butter

Powdered sugar

1. Combine Gouda cheese, cream cheese, honey and cinnamon in small bowl; stir until well blended. Spread cheese mixture evenly on all bread slices. Layer apple slices evenly over cheese on 2 bread slices; top with remaining bread slices.

2. Combine milk and egg in shallow bowl; stir until well blended. Dip sandwiches in egg mixture, turning to coat well.

3. Melt butter in large Red Copper™ Pan over medium heat. Add sandwiches; cook 4 to 5 minutes per side or until cheese is melted and sandwiches are golden brown. Sprinkle with powdered sugar.

MAKES 2 SANDWICHES

Tip: Melting the butter in the Red Copper™ Pan before adding the sandwiches, adds additional buttery flavor.

Baked Apple Pancake

3 tablespoons butter

3 medium Granny Smith apples (about 1¼ pounds), peeled and cut into ¼-inch slices

½ cup packed dark brown sugar

1½ teaspoons ground cinnamon

½ teaspoon plus pinch of salt, divided

4 eggs

⅓ cup whipping cream

⅓ cup milk

2 tablespoons granulated sugar

½ teaspoon vanilla

⅔ cup all-purpose flour

1. Melt butter in Red Copper™ Pan over medium heat. Add apples, brown sugar, cinnamon and pinch of salt; cook about 8 minutes or until apples begin to soften, stirring occasionally. Spread apples in even layer in pan; set aside to cool 30 minutes.

2. After apples have cooled 30 minutes, preheat oven to 425°F. Whisk eggs in large bowl until foamy. Add cream, milk, granulated sugar, vanilla and remaining ½ teaspoon salt; whisk until blended. Sift flour into egg mixture; whisk until batter is well blended and smooth. Set aside 15 minutes.

3. Stir batter; pour evenly over apple mixture. Place pan on rimmed baking sheet in case of drips.

4. Bake about 16 minutes or until top is golden brown and pancake is loose around edge. Cool 1 minute; loosen edge of pancake with spatula, if necessary. Place large serving plate or cutting board on top of pan and invert pancake onto plate. Serve warm.

MAKES 2 TO 4 SERVINGS

Pea and Spinach Frittata

1 cup chopped onion

¼ cup water

1 cup frozen peas

1 cup fresh spinach

6 egg whites

2 eggs

½ cup cooked brown rice

¼ cup milk

2 tablespoons grated Romano or Parmesan cheese, plus additional for garnish

1 tablespoon chopped fresh mint *or* 1 teaspoon dried mint

¼ teaspoon black pepper

⅛ teaspoon salt

1. Combine onion and water in Red Copper™ Pan. Bring to a boil over high heat. Reduce heat to medium. Cover and cook 2 to 3 minutes or until onion is tender. Stir in peas; cook until heated through. Drain. Add spinach; cook and stir 1 minute or until spinach just begins to wilt.

2. Combine egg whites, eggs, rice, milk, 2 tablespoons Romano cheese, mint, pepper and salt in medium bowl. Add egg mixture to pan. Cook, without stirring, 2 minutes until eggs begin to set. Run large spoon around edge of pan, lifting eggs for even cooking. Remove pan from heat when eggs are almost set but surface is still moist.

3. Cover; let stand 3 to 4 minutes or until surface is set. Sprinkle with additional Romano cheese, if desired. Cut into four wedges to serve.

MAKES 4 SERVINGS

Ham and Potato Pancakes

¾ pound Yukon Gold potatoes, peeled, grated and squeezed dry (about 2 cups)

¼ cup finely chopped green onions

2 eggs, beaten

1 cup (4 to 5 ounces) finely chopped cooked ham

¼ cup rice flour

¼ teaspoon salt

¼ teaspoon black pepper

3 tablespoons vegetable oil

Chili sauce or fruit chutney (optional)

1. Combine potatoes, green onions and eggs in large bowl; mix well. Add ham, rice flour, salt and pepper; mix well.

2. Heat 2 tablespoons oil in large Red Copper™ Pan over medium-high heat. Drop batter into pan by heaping tablespoonfuls and press with back of spoon to flatten. Cook 2 to 3 minutes per side. Remove to paper towels to drain. Add remaining 1 tablespoon oil, if necessary, to cook remaining batter. Serve pancakes with chili sauce.

MAKES 16 PANCAKES

Tip: Rice flour can often be substituted for regular all-purpose flour in recipes like this one. If a small amount of flour is called for to bind ingredients together, rice flour works just as well as regular flour. Use either brown or white rice flour. Brown rice flour, like the brown rice it is made from, has a slightly better nutritional profile.

APPETIZERS & SNACKS

Mac & Cheese Bites

3 packages (3 ounces each) ramen noodles, any flavor, divided*

8 ounces pasteurized process cheese product

1 cup (4 ounces) shredded Cheddar cheese

1 teaspoon salt

½ teaspoon ground red pepper

Vegetable oil

*Discard seasoning packets.

1. Prepare 2 packages ramen according to package directions; drain and return to saucepan.

2. Stir in cheese product, Cheddar cheese, salt and ground red pepper. Let stand 10 to 15 minutes.

3. Finely crush remaining packet ramen noodles in food processor or blender. Put crumbs in pie pan. Using hands, shape cheese mixture into 1-inch balls; roll in ramen crumbs. Flatten slightly.

4. Heat about ½ to 1 inch oil in large Red Copper™ Pan. Add bites, a few at a time; cook 1½ minutes per side until golden brown. Remove from pan; drain on paper towels.

MAKES ABOUT 2 DOZEN BITES

Elegant Shrimp Scampi

¼ cup (½ stick) plus
2 tablespoons butter

6 to 8 cloves garlic,
minced

1½ pounds large raw
shrimp (about 16),
peeled and deveined
(with tails on)

6 green onions, thinly
sliced

¼ cup dry white wine

Juice of 1 lemon (about
2 tablespoons)

¼ cup chopped fresh
parsley

Salt and black pepper

Lemon slices (optional)

1. Clarify butter by melting it in large Red Copper™ Pan over low heat. *Do not stir.* Skim off white foam that forms on top. Strain clarified butter through cheesecloth into glass measuring cup to yield ⅓ cup. Discard cheesecloth and milky residue at bottom of pan.

2. Heat clarified butter in large pan over medium heat. Add garlic; cook and stir 1 to 2 minutes or until softened but not browned.

3. Add shrimp, green onions, wine and lemon juice; cook and stir 3 to 4 minutes or until shrimp are pink and opaque. *Do not overcook.*

4. Stir in parsley and season with salt and pepper. Garnish with lemon slices.

MAKES 8 SERVINGS

Spicy BBQ Party Franks

1 tablespoon butter

1 package (1 pound) cocktail franks

⅓ cup cola

⅓ cup ketchup

2 tablespoons hot pepper sauce

2 tablespoons packed dark brown sugar

1 tablespoon cider vinegar

1. Melt butter in medium Red Copper™ Pan over medium heat. Pierce cocktail franks with fork. Add franks to pan; cook until slightly browned.

2. Stir in cola, ketchup, hot pepper sauce, brown sugar and vinegar. Reduce heat to low; cook until sauce is reduced to sticky glaze.

MAKES 6 TO 8 SERVINGS

Quesadilla Grande

2 (8-inch) flour tortillas

2 to 3 large fresh stemmed spinach leaves

2 to 3 slices (about 3 ounces) cooked boneless skinless chicken breast

2 tablespoons salsa

1 tablespoon chopped fresh cilantro

¼ cup (1 ounce) shredded Monterey Jack cheese

2 teaspoons butter or margarine (optional)

1. Place 1 tortilla in large Red Copper™ Pan; cover tortilla with spinach leaves. Place chicken in single layer over spinach. Spoon salsa over chicken. Sprinkle with cilantro; top with cheese. Place remaining tortilla on top, pressing tortilla down so filling becomes compact.

2. Cook over medium heat 4 to 5 minutes or until bottom tortilla is lightly browned. Holding top tortilla in place, gently turn over. Continue cooking 4 minutes or until bottom tortilla is browned and cheese is melted.

3. For a crispier finish, place butter in pan to melt; lift quesadilla to let butter flow into center of pan. Cook 30 seconds. Turn over; continue cooking 30 seconds. Cut into wedges to serve.

MAKES 1 SERVING

Mini Meatballs with Red Pepper Dipping Sauce

1 bottled roasted red pepper, drained and coarsely chopped

2 cloves garlic, divided

¼ cup mayonnaise

⅛ teaspoon red pepper flakes (optional)

¼ pound ground beef

¼ pound ground pork

1 cup plain dry bread crumbs, divided

1 shallot, minced

¼ teaspoon salt

⅛ teaspoon black pepper

1 egg, beaten

¼ cup vegetable oil

1. For Red Pepper Dipping Sauce, place roasted red pepper and 1 clove garlic in blender; blend until smooth. Remove to small bowl; stir in mayonnaise and red pepper flakes, if desired. Set aside.

2. Mince remaining clove garlic. Combine ground beef, ground pork, ¼ cup bread crumbs, shallot, garlic, salt and black pepper in medium bowl. Add egg; blend well.

3. Spread the remaining ¾ cup bread crumbs on large plate. Form meat mixture into 32 to 36 (1-inch) meatballs. Roll meatballs in bread crumbs.

4. Heat oil in Red Copper™ Pan over medium-high heat. Add meatballs in batches; cook 8 minutes, turning frequently until browned on all sides and meatballs are cooked through (160°F). Drain on paper towels. Serve with Red Pepper Dipping Sauce.

MAKES 8 OR 9 SERVINGS

Note: The dipping sauce may be prepared and refrigerated up to 4 hours in advance. Allow the sauce to return to room temperature before serving.

Spicy Chicken Bundles

- 1 pound ground chicken
- 2 teaspoons minced fresh ginger
- 2 cloves garlic, minced
- ¼ teaspoon red pepper flakes
- 3 tablespoons soy sauce
- 1 tablespoon cornstarch
- 1 tablespoon peanut or vegetable oil
- ⅓ cup finely chopped water chestnuts
- ⅓ cup thinly sliced green onions
- ¼ cup chopped peanuts
- 12 large lettuce leaves, such as romaine
- Chinese hot mustard (optional)

1. Combine chicken, ginger, garlic and red pepper flakes in medium bowl. Blend soy sauce into cornstarch in cup until smooth.

2. Heat oil in large Red Copper™ Pan over medium-high heat. Add chicken mixture; cook and stir 2 to 3 minutes until chicken is cooked through.

3. Stir soy sauce mixture; add to pan. Stir-fry 30 seconds or until sauce boils and thickens. Add water chestnuts, green onions and peanuts; heat through.*

4. Divide filling evenly among lettuce leaves; roll up. Secure with toothpicks. Serve warm or at room temperature. Do not let filling stand at room temperature more than 2 hours. Serve with hot mustard.

MAKES 12 APPETIZERS

Filling may be made ahead to this point; cover and refrigerate up to 4 hours. Reheat chicken filling until warm. Proceed as directed in step 4.

Buffalo Chicken Sliders

12 to 16 Hawaiian rolls, sliced through the center, keeping them together as two sheets

1½ cups shredded cooked chicken

1 package (8 ounces) cream cheese

½ cup hot pepper sauce

Dried parsley flakes (optional)

1. Preheat oven to 350°F. Place bottom sheet of rolls in Red Copper™ Square Dance Pan.

2. Combine chicken, cream cheese and hot pepper sauce in medium bowl; stir to blend. Spread chicken mixture over rolls in pan; top with top sheet of rolls.

3. Bake 10 to 12 minutes or until heated through and rolls are browned. Sprinkle with parsley, if desired.

MAKES 4 SERVINGS

Falafel Nuggets

2 cans (about 15 ounces each) chickpeas

½ cup whole wheat flour

½ cup chopped fresh parsley

1 egg, beaten

⅓ cup lemon juice

¼ cup minced onion

2 tablespoons minced garlic

2 teaspoons ground cumin

½ teaspoon salt

½ teaspoon ground red pepper or red pepper flakes

Nonstick cooking spray

Marinara sauce

1. Preheat oven to 400°F.

2. Drain chickpeas, reserving ¼ cup liquid. Combine chickpeas, reserved ¼ cup liquid, flour, parsley, lemon juice, onion, garlic, cumin, salt and ground red pepper in food processor or blender; process until well blended. Shape into 36 (1-inch) balls; place 1 to 2 inches apart in large Red Copper™ Pan. Refrigerate 15 minutes.

3. Remove pan from refrigerator. Spray balls lightly with cooking spray. Bake 15 to 20 minutes, turning once. Serve with warm marinara sauce.

MAKES 12 SERVINGS

Beer Batter Tempura

1½ cups all-purpose flour

1½ cups Japanese beer, chilled

1 teaspoon salt

Dipping Sauce (recipe follows)

Vegetable oil for frying

½ pound green beans or asparagus tips

1 large sweet potato, cut into ¼-inch slices

1 medium eggplant, cut into ¼-inch slices

1. Combine flour, beer and salt in medium bowl just until mixed. Batter should be thin and lumpy. *Do not overmix.* Let stand 15 minutes. Meanwhile, prepare Dipping Sauce.

2. Heat 1 inch oil in large Red Copper™ Pan to 375°F; adjust heat to maintain temperature.

3. Dip 10 to 12 green beans in batter; add to hot oil. Fry until light golden brown. Remove to wire racks or paper towels to drain; keep warm. Repeat with remaining vegetables, working with only one vegetable at a time and being careful not to crowd vegetables. Serve with Dipping Sauce.

MAKES 4 SERVINGS

Dipping Sauce

½ cup soy sauce

2 tablespoons rice wine

1 tablespoon sugar

½ teaspoon white vinegar

2 teaspoons minced fresh ginger

1 clove garlic, minced

2 green onions, thinly sliced

Combine soy sauce, rice wine, sugar and vinegar in small saucepan; cook and stir over medium heat 3 minutes or until sugar dissolves. Add ginger and garlic; cook and stir 2 minutes. Stir in green onions; remove from heat.

MAKES ABOUT 1 CUP

Chicken Bacon Quesadillas

4 teaspoons vegetable oil, divided

4 (8-inch) flour tortillas

1 cup (4 ounces) shredded Colby-Jack cheese

2 cups coarsely chopped cooked chicken

4 slices bacon, crisp-cooked and coarsely chopped

½ cup pico de gallo

Salsa, sour cream and guacamole

1. Heat large Red Copper™ Pan over medium heat; brush with 1 teaspoon oil. Place 1 tortilla in pan; sprinkle with ¼ cup cheese. Spread ½ cup chicken over one half of tortilla; top with one fourth of bacon and 2 tablespoons pico de gallo.

2. Cook 1 to 2 minutes or until cheese is melted and bottom of tortilla is lightly browned. Fold tortilla over filling, pressing with spatula. Transfer to cutting board; cool slightly. Cut into wedges. Repeat with remaining ingredients. Serve with salsa, sour cream and guacamole.

MAKES 4 SERVINGS

Chicken Nuggets with Spicy Tomato Dipping Sauce

Spicy Tomato Dipping Sauce (recipe follows)

½ cup panko bread crumbs

½ cup grated Parmesan cheese

1 package (3 ounces) ramen noodles, any flavor, finely crushed*

1 teaspoon garlic powder

1 teaspoon dried basil

½ teaspoon salt

¼ teaspoon black pepper

1 egg, lightly beaten

1½ pounds boneless skinless chicken breasts, cut into 1×2½-inch pieces

½ cup vegetable oil

*Discard seasoning packet.

1. Prepare Spicy Tomato Dipping Sauce; set aside. Combine panko, cheese, noodles, garlic powder, basil, salt and pepper in large bowl. Place egg in shallow dish. Dip chicken in egg; shake off excess. Coat with panko mixture.

2. Heat oil in large Red Copper™ Pan over medium heat. Cook chicken in batches about 5 minutes or until cooked through, turning once. Serve with Spicy Tomato Dipping Sauce.

MAKES 4 SERVINGS

Spicy Tomato Dipping Sauce

1 tablespoon olive oil

1 small onion, chopped

2 cloves garlic, minced

¼ teaspoon ground red pepper

1 can (about 14 ounces) fire-roasted diced tomatoes

1. Heat oil in medium Red Copper™ Pan. Add onion and garlic; cook and stir about 3 minutes or until onion is tender and golden brown. Stir in ground red pepper.

2. Remove pan from heat; add tomatoes. Process in blender or food processor until smooth. Return to pan and cook about 10 minutes or until thickened and reduced to 1½ cups.

MAKES 1½ CUPS

DINNERTIME
FAVORITES

Emerald Isle Lamb Chops

2 tablespoons vegetable or olive oil, divided

2 tablespoons coarse Dijon mustard

1 tablespoon Irish whiskey

1 tablespoon minced fresh rosemary

2 teaspoons minced garlic

1½ pounds loin lamb chops (about 6 chops)

½ teaspoon salt

½ teaspoon black pepper

¾ cup dry white wine

2 tablespoons black currant jam

1 to 2 tablespoons butter, cut into small pieces

1. Combine 1 tablespoon oil, mustard, whiskey, rosemary and garlic in small bowl to form paste. Season lamb chops with salt and pepper; spread paste over both sides. Cover and marinate 30 minutes at room temperature or refrigerate 2 to 3 hours.

2. Heat remaining 1 tablespoon oil in large Red Copper™ Pan over medium-high heat. Add lamb chops in single layer; cook 2 to 3 minutes per side or until desired doneness. Remove to serving plate and keep warm.

3. Drain excess fat from pan. Add wine; cook and stir about 5 minutes, scraping up brown bits from bottom of pan. Stir in jam until well blended. Remove from heat; stir in butter until melted. Serve sauce over lamb chops.

MAKES 4 TO 6 SERVINGS

Pan-Fried Cajun Bass

2 tablespoons all-purpose flour

1 to 1½ teaspoons Cajun or Caribbean jerk seasoning

1 egg white

2 teaspoons water

⅓ cup seasoned dry bread crumbs

2 tablespoons cornmeal

4 skinless striped bass, halibut or cod fillets (4 to 6 ounces each), thawed if frozen

1 teaspoon butter

1 teaspoon olive oil

Chopped fresh parsley (optional)

4 lemon wedges

1. Combine flour and seasoning in medium resealable food storage bag. Beat egg white and water in small bowl. Combine bread crumbs and cornmeal in separate small bowl.

2. Working one at a time, add fillet to bag; shake to coat evenly. Dip in egg white mixture, letting excess drip back into bowl. Roll in bread crumb mixture, pressing lightly to adhere. Repeat with remaining fillets.

3. Melt butter and oil in large Red Copper™ Pan over medium heat. Add fillets; cook 4 to 5 minutes per side or until golden brown and fish is opaque in center and flakes easily when tested with fork.

4. Sprinkle parsley over fish, if desired. Serve with lemon wedges.

MAKES 4 SERVINGS

Bacon-Crusted Hawaiian Pizza

1 package refrigerated pizza dough

8 slices bacon, crisp-cooked

¼ cup pizza or marinara sauce

Ham or Canadian bacon, thinly sliced

1 small green bell pepper, thinly sliced

1 can (8 ounces) pineapple tidbits, drained

Shredded mozzarella cheese

1. Preheat oven to 350°F. Place pizza dough in Red Copper™ Square Dance Pan; press dough on bottom and slightly up sides of pan.

2. Place bacon around edges of pan; pressing bacon into dough. Spread sauce over dough; top with ham, bell pepper and pineapple. Top with cheese.

3. Bake 15 to 20 minutes or until crust is brown and cheese is melted.

MAKES 6 SERVINGS

Veggie-Packed Spaghetti & Meatballs

4 ounces uncooked spaghetti or vermicelli

¾ pound lean ground turkey or beef

1 package (10 ounces) frozen chopped spinach, thawed and pressed dry

½ cup fresh whole wheat bread crumbs*

1 egg white

1 teaspoon onion powder

1 teaspoon garlic powder

½ teaspoon black pepper

2 cups pasta sauce

2 cups (5 ounces) small broccoli florets

½ cup packaged julienned carrots

*To make fresh bread crumbs, tear 1 slice bread into pieces; process in food processor until coarse crumbs form.

1. Cook spaghetti according to package directions, omitting salt. Drain.

2. Meanwhile, combine turkey, spinach, bread crumbs, egg white, onion powder, garlic powder and pepper in medium bowl; mix well. Shape into 32 (½-inch) meatballs.

3. Heat large Red Copper™ Pan over medium heat. Add meatballs; cook 8 to 10 minutes, turning to brown all sides.

4. Add pasta sauce, broccoli and carrots to pan. Cover; bring to a simmer over medium-low heat. Cook 8 to 10 or until vegetables are tender and sauce is heated through.

5. Spoon sauce and meatballs evenly over spaghetti.

MAKES 4 SERVINGS

Curried Quinoa Burgers

½ cup quinoa, rinsed well in fine mesh strainer

½ cup red lentils, rinsed well in fine mesh strainer

1½ cups water

3 tablespoons olive oil, divided

1 medium onion, diced

1 teaspoon kosher salt

½ cup frozen peas

3 cloves garlic, minced

2 teaspoons curry powder

1 egg

6 hamburger buns

Lettuce, sliced tomatoes, thinly sliced red onion, mango chutney (optional)

1. Combine quinoa, lentils and water in large Red Copper™ Pan over medium-high heat; bring to a boil. Reduce heat to low; cover and cook 15 minutes or until quinoa is cooked and lentils are tender. Remove to large bowl.

2. Heat 1 tablespoon oil in large same pan over medium-high heat. Add onion and salt; cook 6 minutes or until onion begins to soften. Reduce heat to medium; add peas; cook 4 minutes. Add garlic and curry powder; cook 30 seconds, stirring frequently. Add to quinoa mixture with egg; stir until combined. Cool mixture 15 minutes.

3. Portion out ½-cup mixture into individual patties about ½×½ inch thick.

4. Heat 1 tablespoon oil in pan over medium-high heat. Reduce heat to medium; gently place patties in pan. Cook 4 to 5 minutes or until well browned on bottom. Add remaining 1 tablespoon oil to pan; flip patties and continue cooking 4 to 5 minutes or until browned on other side.

5. Place burgers on buns. Top as desired.

MAKES 6 SERVINGS

Sweet and Sour Chicken

1 pound chicken tenders, cut into 1-inch pieces

⅓ cup plus 2 tablespoons cornstarch, divided

Salt and black pepper

¼ cup ketchup

¼ cup packed brown sugar

1 can (8 ounces) pineapple tidbits, drained with juice reserved

2 tablespoons vegetable oil

1 large green bell pepper, cut into 1-inch squares

½ medium onion, chopped

Hot cooked rice

1. Place chicken, ⅓ cup cornstarch, salt and black pepper in large resealable food storage bag; shake to coat. Combine ketchup, brown sugar and remaining 2 tablespoons cornstarch in medium bowl; stir to blend. Add enough water to reserved pineapple juice to measure 1 cup; stir into ketchup mixture.

2. Heat oil in large Red Copper™ Pan over medium-high heat. Add chicken, shaking off excess cornstarch mixture; cook and stir 6 minutes or until browned. Add bell pepper and onion; cook 6 minutes or until softened. Pour ketchup mixture over chicken; cook and stir 6 minutes or until thickened. Stir in pineapple tidbits. Serve over rice.

MAKES 4 SERVINGS

Pumpkin Curry

1 tablespoon vegetable oil

1 package (14 ounces) extra firm tofu, drained and cut into 1-inch cubes

¼ cup Thai red curry paste

2 cloves garlic, minced

1 can (15 ounces) solid-pack pumpkin

1 can (14 ounces) coconut milk

1 cup water

1½ teaspoons salt

1 teaspoon sriracha sauce

4 cups cut-up vegetables (broccoli, cauliflower, red bell pepper, sweet potato)

½ cup peas

2 cups hot cooked rice

¼ cup shredded fresh basil (optional)

1. Heat oil in large Red Copper™ Pan over high heat. Add tofu; stir-fry 2 to 3 minutes or until lightly browned. Add curry paste and garlic; cook and stir 1 minute or until tofu is coated. Add pumpkin, coconut milk, water, salt and sriracha; bring to a boil. Stir in vegetables.

2. Reduce heat to medium; cover and simmer 20 minutes or until vegetables are tender. Stir in peas; cook 1 minute or until heated through. Serve over rice; top with basil, if desired.

MAKES 4 SERVINGS

Blackened Shrimp with Tomatoes

1½ teaspoons paprika

1 teaspoon Italian seasoning

½ teaspoon garlic powder

¼ teaspoon black pepper

½ pound (about 24) small raw shrimp, peeled (with tails on)

1 tablespoon canola oil

½ cup sliced red onion, separated into rings

1½ cups halved grape tomatoes

Lime wedges (optional)

1. Combine paprika, Italian seasoning, garlic powder and pepper in large resealable food storage bag. Add shrimp; seal bag and shake to coat.

2. Heat oil in large Red Copper™ Pan over medium-high heat. Add shrimp; cook 4 minutes or until shrimp are pink and opaque, turning occasionally. Add onion and tomatoes; cook 1 minute or until tomatoes are heated through and onion is softened. Serve with lime wedges, if desired.

MAKES 4 SERVINGS

Easy Chicken Parmesan

1 tablespoon olive oil

4 boneless skinless chicken breasts

1 medium onion, chopped

1 small zucchini, sliced

1 jar (26 ounces) pasta sauce

½ teaspoon dried basil

½ teaspoon dried oregano

8 ounces fresh mozzarella cheese, cut into thin slices

¼ cup grated Parmesan cheese

Hot cooked spaghetti

1. Preheat broiler.

2. Heat oil in large Red Copper™ Pan over medium-high heat. Add chicken; cook 5 to 7 minutes or until browned on both sides. Add onion and zucchini; cook 5 minutes or until vegetables are softened. Stir in pasta sauce, basil and oregano. Top chicken with mozzarella slices.

3. Broil 6 inches from heat 5 to 7 minutes or until chicken is no longer pink in center and cheese is beginning to brown. Sprinkle each serving with Parmesan cheese and serve over spaghetti.

MAKES 4 SERVINGS

Grilled 3-Cheese Sandwiches

2 slices (1 ounce each) Muenster cheese

2 slices (1 ounce each) Swiss cheese

2 slices (1 ounce each) Cheddar cheese

2 teaspoons Dijon mustard or Dijon mustard mayonnaise

4 slices sourdough bread

2 teaspoons melted butter

1. Place 1 slice of each cheese on 2 bread slices. Spread mustard over cheese; top with remaining bread slices. Brush outsides of sandwiches with butter.

2. Heat large Red Copper™ Pan over medium heat. Add sandwiches; press down lightly with spatula or weigh down with small plate. Cook 4 minutes per side or until cheese is melted and sandwiches are golden brown.

MAKES 2 SANDWICHES

Beef and Broccoli

1 pound beef tenderloin steaks

2 teaspoons minced fresh ginger

2 cloves garlic, minced

½ teaspoon vegetable oil

3 cups broccoli florets

¼ cup water

2 tablespoons teriyaki sauce

2 cups hot cooked rice

1. Cut beef crosswise into ⅛-inch-thick slices. Toss beef with ginger and garlic in medium bowl.

2. Heat oil in Red Copper™ Pan over medium heat. Add half of beef mixture; stir-fry 2 to 3 minutes or until beef is barely pink in center. Remove to medium bowl. Repeat with remaining beef.

3. Add broccoli and water to pan; cover and steam 3 to 5 minutes or until broccoli is crisp-tender.

4. Return beef and any accumulated juices to pan. Add teriyaki sauce; cook until heated through. Serve over rice.

MAKES 4 SERVINGS

Sassy Chicken & Peppers

2 teaspoons Mexican seasoning*

2 boneless skinless chicken breasts (about ¼ pound each)

2 teaspoons vegetable oil

1 small red onion, sliced

½ medium red bell pepper, cut into thin strips

½ medium yellow or green bell pepper, cut into thin strips

¼ cup chunky salsa or chipotle salsa

1 tablespoon lime juice

Lime wedges (optional)

*If Mexican seasoning is not available, substitute 1 teaspoon chili powder, ½ teaspoon ground cumin, ½ teaspoon salt and ⅛ teaspoon ground red pepper.

1. Sprinkle seasoning over both sides of chicken; set aside.

2. Heat oil in large Red Copper™ Pan over medium heat. Add onion; cook 3 minutes, stirring occasionally.

3. Add bell peppers; cook 3 minutes, stirring occasionally. Stir salsa and lime juice into vegetables.

4. Push vegetables to edge of pan. Add chicken to pan. Cook 5 minutes; turn. Continue to cook 4 minutes or until chicken is no longer pink in center and vegetables are tender.

5. Transfer chicken to serving plates; top with vegetable mixture. Garnish with lime wedges.

MAKES 2 SERVINGS

Crispy Buttermilk Fried Chicken

2 cups buttermilk

1 tablespoon hot pepper sauce

3 pounds bone-in chicken pieces

2 cups all-purpose flour

2 teaspoons salt

2 teaspoons poultry seasoning

1 teaspoon garlic salt

1 teaspoon paprika

1 teaspoon ground red pepper

1 teaspoon black pepper

1 cup vegetable oil

1. Combine buttermilk and hot pepper sauce in large resealable food storage bag. Add chicken; seal bag. Turn to coat; refrigerate 2 hours or up to 24 hours.

2. Combine flour, salt, poultry seasoning, garlic salt, paprika, ground red pepper and black pepper in another large resealable food storage bag or shallow baking dish; blend well. Working in batches, remove chicken from buttermilk; shake off excess. Add to flour mixture; shake to coat.

3. Heat oil over medium heat in large Red Copper™ Pan until deep-fry thermometer registers 350°F. Working in batches, fry chicken 30 minutes or until cooked through (165°F), turning occasionally to brown all sides. Drain on paper towels.

MAKES 4 SERVINGS

Note: Carefully monitor the temperature of the oil during cooking. It should not drop below 325°F or go higher than 350°F.

SIZZLING
SIDE DISHES

Tangy Red Cabbage with Apples and Bacon

8 slices thick-cut bacon

1 large onion, sliced

½ small head red cabbage (1 pound), thinly sliced

1 tablespoon sugar

1 Granny Smith apple, peeled and sliced

2 tablespoons cider vinegar

½ teaspoon salt

¼ teaspoon black pepper

1. Heat large Red Copper™ Pan over medium-high heat. Add bacon; cook 6 to 8 minutes or until crisp, turning occasionally. Drain on paper towel-lined plate. Coarsely chop bacon.

2. Drain all but 2 tablespoons drippings from pan. Add onion; cook and stir over medium-high heat 2 to 3 minutes or until onion begins to soften. Add cabbage and sugar; cook and stir 4 to 5 minutes or until cabbage wilts. Stir in apple; cook 3 minutes or until crisp-tender. Stir in vinegar; cook 1 minute or until absorbed.

3. Stir in bacon, salt and pepper; cook 1 minute or until heated through. Serve hot or at room temperature.

MAKES 4 SERVINGS

Charred Corn Salad

3 tablespoons fresh lime juice

½ teaspoon salt

¼ cup extra virgin olive oil

4 to 6 ears corn, husked (enough to make 3 to 4 cups kernels)

⅔ cup canned black beans, rinsed and drained

½ cup chopped fresh cilantro

2 teaspoons minced seeded chipotle pepper (1 canned chipotle pepper in adobo sauce *or* 1 dried chipotle pepper, reconstituted in boiling water)*

*Chipotle peppers can sting and irritate the skin, so wear rubber gloves when handling peppers and do not touch your eyes.

1. Whisk lime juice and salt in small bowl. Gradually whisk in oil. Set aside.

2. Heat large Red Copper™ Pan over medium-high heat. Cook corn in single layer 15 to 17 minutes or until browned and tender, turning frequently. Transfer to plate to cool slightly. Place in medium bowl.

3. Microwave beans in small microwavable bowl on HIGH 1 minute or until heated through. Add beans, cilantro and chipotle pepper to corn; mix well. Pour lime juice mixture over corn mixture; toss to combine.

MAKES 6 SERVINGS

Note: Chipotle peppers in adobo sauce are available canned in the Mexican food section of most supermarkets. Since only a small amount is needed for this dish, spoon leftovers into a covered plastic container and refrigerate or freeze.

Cantonese Rice Cake Patties

2 cups cooked rice, chilled

⅓ cup chopped red bell pepper

¼ cup thinly sliced green onions

2 egg whites, lightly beaten

1 egg, lightly beaten

2 tablespoons soy sauce

2 tablespoons vegetable oil

1. Combine rice, bell pepper, green onions, egg whites, egg and soy sauce in medium bowl; mix well.

2. Heat 1 tablespoon oil in large Red Copper™ Pan over medium heat. Spoon ⅓ cupfuls rice mixture into pan; flatten slightly with back of spatula. Cook 3 to 4 minutes per side or until golden brown.* Repeat with remaining 1 tablespoon oil and rice mixture.

*To keep warm while preparing remaining patties, place on large baking sheet in 200°F oven.

MAKES ABOUT 9 PATTIES

Caramelized Brussels Sprouts with Cranberries

1 tablespoon vegetable oil

1 pound Brussels sprouts, ends trimmed and discarded, thinly sliced

¼ cup dried cranberries

2 teaspoons packed brown sugar

¼ teaspoon salt

Heat oil in large Red Copper™ Pan over medium-high heat. Add Brussels sprouts; cook and stir 10 minutes or until crisp-tender and beginning to brown. Add cranberries, brown sugar and salt; cook and stir 5 minutes or until browned.

MAKES 4 SERVINGS

Fried Green Tomatoes

2 medium green tomatoes

¼ cup all-purpose flour

¼ cup yellow cornmeal

½ teaspoon salt

½ teaspoon garlic salt

½ teaspoon ground red pepper

½ teaspoon cracked black pepper

1 cup buttermilk

1 cup vegetable oil

Hot pepper sauce (optional)

1. Cut tomatoes into ¼-inch-thick slices. Combine flour, cornmeal, salt, garlic salt, ground red pepper and black pepper in pie plate or shallow bowl; mix well. Pour buttermilk into second pie plate or shallow bowl.

2. Heat oil in large Red Copper™ Pan over medium heat. Dip tomato slices into buttermilk, coating both sides. Immediately dredge slices in flour mixture; shake off excess flour mixture.

3. Cook tomato slices in hot oil 3 to 5 minutes per side. Transfer to paper towels. Serve immediately with hot pepper sauce, if desired.

MAKES 3 TO 4 SERVINGS

Serving Suggestion: Serve fried green tomatoes on a bed of shredded lettuce.

Chinese Vegetables

1 pound fresh broccoli

1½ teaspoons vegetable oil

2 medium yellow onions, cut into wedges and separated

2 cloves garlic, minced

1½ tablespoons minced fresh ginger

8 ounces fresh spinach, coarsely chopped

4 stalks celery, diagonally cut into ½-inch pieces

8 ounces fresh snow peas *or* 1 package (6 ounces) thawed frozen snow peas, trimmed and strings removed

4 medium carrots, sliced

8 green onions, diagonally cut into thin slices

¾ cup chicken broth

1 tablespoon soy sauce

Hot cooked rice

1. Cut broccoli tops into florets. Cut stalks into 2×¼-inch strips.

2. Heat oil in large Red Copper™ Pan over high heat. Add broccoli stalks, yellow onions, garlic and ginger; stir-fry 1 minute. Add broccoli florets, spinach, celery, snow peas, carrots and green onions; toss lightly.

3. Add broth and soy sauce to vegetables; toss to coat. Bring to a boil; cover and cook 2 to 3 minutes or until vegetables are crisp-tender. Serve over rice.

MAKES 6 TO 8 SIDE-DISH SERVINGS

Dry-Cooked Green Beans

4 ounces lean ground
   pork or turkey

2 tablespoons plus
   1 teaspoon light soy
   sauce, divided

2 tablespoons plus
   1 teaspoon rice wine or
   dry sherry, divided

½ teaspoon dark sesame
   oil

2 tablespoons water

1 teaspoon sugar

3 cups vegetable oil

1 pound fresh green
   beans, trimmed and
   cut into 2-inch lengths

1 tablespoon sliced green
   onion

1. Combine pork, 1 teaspoon soy sauce, 1 teaspoon rice wine and sesame oil in medium bowl; mix well. Set aside.

2. Combine water, sugar, remaining 2 tablespoons soy sauce and 2 tablespoons rice wine in small bowl; mix well. Set aside.

3. Heat vegetable oil in large Red Copper™ Pan over medium-high heat until oil registers 375°F on deep-fry thermometer. Carefully add ½ of beans and fry 2 to 3 minutes or until beans blister and are crisp-tender. Remove beans with slotted spoon to paper towels; drain. When oil returns to 375°F, repeat with remaining beans.

4. Pour off oil; heat pan over medium-high heat 30 seconds. Add pork mixture and stir-fry about 2 minutes or until well browned. Add beans and soy sauce mixture; toss until heated through. Transfer to serving dish. Sprinkle with green onion.

MAKES 4 SERVINGS

Southern-Style Succotash

2 tablespoons butter

1 cup chopped onion

1 package (10 ounces) frozen lima beans, thawed

1 cup frozen corn, thawed

½ cup chopped red bell pepper

1 can (about 15 ounces) hominy, rinsed and drained

⅓ cup chicken broth

¼ teaspoon hot pepper sauce

¼ cup chopped green onion tops or fresh chives

1. Melt butter in large Red Copper™ Pan over medium heat. Add onion; cook and stir 5 minutes. Add lima beans, corn and bell pepper; cook and stir 5 minutes.

2. Add hominy, broth and hot pepper sauce; simmer 5 minutes or until most liquid is evaporated. Remove from heat; stir in chopped green onions before serving.

MAKES 6 SERVINGS

Hot and Sour Zucchini

2 teaspoons minced fresh ginger

1 clove garlic, minced

¼ teaspoon red pepper flakes or crushed Szechuan peppercorns

1 pound zucchini

2 teaspoons sugar

1 teaspoon cornstarch

2 tablespoons red wine vinegar

2 tablespoons soy sauce

1 tablespoon peanut or vegetable oil

1 teaspoon dark sesame oil

1. Combine ginger, garlic and red pepper flakes in small bowl. Cut zucchini into ¼-inch slices. If zucchini is large, cut each slice in half. Toss zucchini with ginger mixture.

2. Combine sugar and cornstarch in small bowl. Stir in vinegar and soy sauce until smooth.

3. Heat large Red Copper™ Pan over medium-high heat. Add peanut oil; heat until hot. Add zucchini mixture; stir-fry 4 to 5 minutes until zucchini is crisp-tender.

4. Stir vinegar mixture and add to pan. Stir-fry 15 seconds or until sauce boils and thickens. Stir in sesame oil.

MAKES 4 SERVINGS

Sesame Snow Peas

½ pound snow peas
(Chinese pea pods)

2 teaspoons dark sesame
oil

2 teaspoons vegetable oil

1 medium carrot, cut into
matchstick pieces

2 green onions, cut into
¼-inch slices

½ teaspoon grated fresh
ginger *or* ¼ teaspoon
ground ginger

1 teaspoon soy sauce

1 tablespoon sesame
seeds, toasted*

*To toast sesame seeds, heat
small pan over medium heat.
Add sesame seeds; cook and stir
about 5 minutes or until golden.*

1. To de-stem peas, pinch off stem end from each pod and pull strings down pod to remove, if present. (Young tender pods may have no strings.)

2. To stir-fry, place large Red Copper™ Pan over high heat. Add sesame and vegetable oils; heat oil 30 seconds. Add snow peas, carrot, green onions and ginger; stir-fry 4 minutes or until peas are bright green and crisp-tender.

3. Stir in soy sauce. Transfer to warm serving dish; sprinkle with sesame seeds. Serve immediately.

MAKES 4 SIDE-DISH SERVINGS

Square Dance Corn Casserole

1 box (about 8 ounces) corn bread mix

1 can (15 ounces) corn, drained

1 can (15 ounces) creamed corn

½ cup sour cream

½ cup (1 stick) butter, melted

1 can (4 ounces) diced mild green chiles (optional)

1. Preheat oven to 350°F.

2. Combine corn bread mix, corn, creamed corn, sour cream, butter and chiles, if desired, in Red Copper™ Square Dance Pan; stir to blend.

3. Bake 45 minutes or until lightly browned.

MAKES 6 SERVINGS

Asparagus with No-Cook Creamy Mustard Sauce

2 cups water

1½ pounds asparagus, trimmed

½ cup plain yogurt

2 tablespoons mayonnaise

1 tablespoon Dijon mustard

2 teaspoons lemon juice

½ teaspoon salt

Grated lemon peel (optional)

1. Bring water to a boil in large Red Copper™ Pan over high heat. Add asparagus; return to a boil. Reduce heat; cover and simmer 3 minutes or until crisp-tender. Drain.

2. Meanwhile, whisk yogurt, mayonnaise, mustard, lemon juice and salt in small bowl until smooth and well blended.

3. Place asparagus on serving platter; top with sauce. Garnish with lemon peel.

MAKES 6 SERVINGS

Country-Style Corn

4 slices bacon

1 tablespoon all-purpose flour

1 can (about 15 ounces) corn, drained

1 can (about 15 ounces) cream-style corn

1 red bell pepper, diced

½ cup sliced green onions

Salt and black pepper

1. Cook bacon in large Red Copper™ Pan over medium heat until crisp; drain on paper towels. Crumble bacon; set aside.

2. Whisk flour into drippings in pan. Add corn, cream-style corn and bell pepper; bring to a boil. Reduce heat to low. Cook 10 minutes or until thickened.

3. Stir green onions and bacon into corn mixture. Season with salt and black pepper.

MAKES 6 TO 8 SERVINGS

Green Beans and Shiitake Mushrooms

10 to 12 dried shiitake mushrooms (about 1 ounce)

¾ cup water, divided

3 tablespoons oyster sauce

1 tablespoon cornstarch

4 cloves garlic, minced

⅛ teaspoon red pepper flakes

1 tablespoon vegetable oil

¾ to 1 pound fresh green beans, ends trimmed

⅓ cup slivered fresh basil or chopped fresh cilantro

2 green onions, sliced diagonally

⅓ cup roasted peanuts

1. Place mushrooms in bowl; cover with hot water. Let stand 30 minutes or until caps are soft. Drain mushrooms; squeeze out excess water. Remove and discard stems. Slice caps into thin strips.

2. Combine ¼ cup water, oyster sauce, cornstarch, garlic and red pepper flakes in small bowl; mix well. Set aside.

3. Heat oil in medium Red Copper™ Pan over medium-high heat. Add mushrooms, beans and remaining ½ cup water; cook and stir until water boils. Reduce heat to medium-low; cover and cook 8 to 10 minutes or until beans are crisp-tender, stirring occasionally.

4. Stir cornstarch mixture; add to pan. Cook and stir until sauce thickens and coats beans. (If cooking water has evaporated, add enough water to form thick sauce.) Stir in basil, green onions and peanuts; mix well. Transfer to serving platter.

MAKES 4 TO 6 SERVINGS

DELICIOUS DESSERTS

Sautéed Apples Supreme

2 small apples *or* 1 large apple

1 teaspoon butter

¼ cup unsweetened apple juice or cider

2 teaspoons packed brown sugar

½ teaspoon ground cinnamon

Vanilla ice cream

2 tablespoons chopped walnuts, toasted*

To toast walnuts, spread in single layer in pan. Cook and stir over medium heat 1 to 2 minutes or until nuts are lightly browned.

1. Cut apples into quarters; remove cores and cut into ½-inch-thick slices.

2. Melt butter in large Red Copper™ Pan over medium heat. Add apples; cook 4 minutes, stirring occasionally.

3. Combine apple juice, brown sugar and cinnamon in small bowl; pour over apples. Simmer 5 minutes or until apples are tender and sauce thickens. Serve over ice cream; sprinkle with walnuts.

MAKES 2 SERVINGS

Cinnamon Dessert Tacos with Fruit Salsa

1 cup sliced fresh strawberries

1 cup cubed fresh pineapple

1 cup cubed peeled kiwi

½ teaspoon minced jalapeno pepper* (optional)

4 tablespoons sugar, divided

1 tablespoon ground cinnamon

6 (8-inch) flour tortillas

Nonstick cooking spray

Jalapeno peppers can sting and irritate the skin, so wear rubber gloves when handling peppers and do not touch your eyes.

1. Stir together strawberries, pineapple, kiwi, jalapeño pepper and 1 tablespoon sugar in large bowl; set aside. Combine remaining 3 tablespoons sugar and cinnamon in small bowl; set aside.

2. Spray tortilla lightly on both sides with cooking spray. Heat over medium heat in medium Red Copper™ Pan until slightly puffed and golden brown. Remove from heat; immediately dust both sides with cinnamon-sugar mixture. Shake excess cinnamon-sugar back into bowl. Repeat until all tortillas are warmed.

3. Fill tortillas with fruit mixture; fold in half. Serve immediately.

MAKES 6 SERVINGS

Poached Pears in Cinnamon-Apricot Sauce

1 can (5½ ounces) apricot nectar

1 tablespoon sugar

1 teaspoon lemon juice

½ teaspoon ground cinnamon

¼ teaspoon grated lemon peel

⅛ teaspoon ground cloves

2 large pears

Whipped topping (optional)

1. Combine apricot nectar, sugar, lemon juice, cinnamon, lemon peel and cloves in large Red Copper™ Pan. Bring to a boil over medium-high heat.

2. Meanwhile, cut pears lengthwise into halves, leaving stem attached to one half. Remove cores. Cut pears lengthwise into thin slices, taking care not to cut through stem end. Add pears to pan with nectar mixture; return to a boil. Reduce heat to medium-low. Simmer, covered, 6 to 8 minutes or just until pears are tender. Carefully remove pears from pan, reserving liquid.

3. Simmer liquid in pan, uncovered, over medium heat 2 to 3 minutes or until mixture thickens slightly, stirring occasionally. Fan out pears; spoon sauce over pears. Serve pears warm or chilled with whipped topping, if desired.

MAKES 4 SERVINGS

Chocolate Chip Skillet Cookie

1¾ cups all-purpose flour

1 teaspoon baking soda

1 teaspoon salt

¾ cup (1½ sticks) butter, softened

¾ cup packed brown sugar

½ cup granulated sugar

2 eggs

1 teaspoon vanilla

1 package (12 ounces) semisweet chocolate chips

Sea salt (optional)

Ice cream (optional)

1. Preheat oven to 350°F.

2. Combine flour, baking soda and salt in medium bowl. Beat butter, brown sugar and granulated sugar in large bowl with electric mixer at medium speed until creamy. Beat in eggs and vanilla until well blended. Gradually beat in flour mixture at low speed just until blended. Stir in chocolate chips. Press batter evenly into large Red Copper™ Pan. Sprinkle lightly with sea salt, if desired.

3. Bake 35 minutes or until top and edges are golden brown but cookie is still soft in center. Cool on wire rack 10 minutes before cutting into wedges. Serve warm with ice cream, if desired.

MAKES 8 SERVINGS

Apple Fritter Cake Squares

- ⅓ cup packed light brown sugar
- 2 teaspoons ground cinnamon, divided
- ½ cup walnuts or pecans, coarsely chopped
- ⅔ cup sugar
- ½ cup (1 stick) butter, softened
- 2 eggs
- 1 teaspoon vanilla
- 1½ cups all-purpose flour
- 2 teaspoons baking powder
- ½ cup plus 1 tablespoon milk, divided
- 2 apples, peeled and chopped
- ½ cup powdered sugar

1. Preheat oven to 350°F. Combine brown sugar, 1 teaspoon cinnamon and walnuts in small bowl; toss to coat. Set aside.

2. Combine sugar and butter in large bowl; beat with electric mixer at medium-high speed 3 to 5 minutes or until blended and fluffy. Add eggs and vanilla; beat until smooth. Combine flour and baking powder in medium bowl; stir to blend. Beat flour mixture into butter mixture alternately with ½ cup milk.

3. Toss apples with remaining 1 teaspoon cinnamon. Stir apples into batter; pour into Red Copper™ Square Dance Pan. Sprinkle reserved brown sugar mixture over top; swirl batter with back of spoon.

4. Bake 40 to 45 minutes or until well browned. Meanwhile, whisk powdered sugar and 1 tablespoon milk in small bowl until smooth and well blended. Pour glaze over cake; cool completely. Cut into nine squares.

MAKES 9 SERVINGS

Honey Sopaipillas

¼ cup plus 2 teaspoons sugar, divided

½ teaspoon ground cinnamon

2 cups all-purpose flour

½ teaspoon salt

2 teaspoons baking powder

2 tablespoons shortening

¾ cup warm water

Vegetable oil for deep-frying

Honey

1. Combine ¼ cup sugar and cinnamon in small bowl; set aside. Combine remaining 2 teaspoons sugar, flour, salt and baking powder in large bowl. Cut in shortening with pastry blender or two knives until mixture resembles fine crumbs. Gradually add water; stir with fork until mixture forms dough. Turn out onto lightly floured surface; knead 2 minutes or until smooth. Shape into a ball; cover with bowl and let rest 30 minutes.

2. Divide dough into four equal portions; shape each into a ball. Flatten each ball into 8-inch circle ⅛ inch thick. Cut each round into four wedges.

3. Pour oil into large Red Copper™ Pan to depth of 1½ inches. Heat to 360°F. Cook dough, two pieces at a time, 2 minutes or until puffed and golden brown, turning once during cooking. Remove from oil with slotted spoon; drain on paper towels. Sprinkle with cinnamon-sugar mixture. Repeat with remaining sopaipillas. Serve hot with honey.

MAKES 16 SOPAIPILLAS

Bananas Foster Sundae

1 medium banana

2 tablespoons packed
brown sugar

2 teaspoons butter

1 tablespoon water

1 teaspoon rum extract

2 cups vanilla ice cream

Wafer cookie pieces
(optional)

1. Peel bananas; cut into ¼-inch slices.

2. Heat brown sugar and butter in medium Red Copper™ Pan over medium-low heat, stirring constantly. Stir in water; cook and stir 30 to 45 seconds or until slightly thickened. Add bananas and rum extract, stirring gently to coat in caramel mixture. Cook about 30 seconds more or until bananas are heated through. Remove from heat.

3. Scoop ice cream into four individual dessert dishes; spoon banana mixture evenly over ice cream. Garnish with wafer cookie pieces. Serve immediately.

MAKES 4 SERVINGS

Chocolate Crêpes with Strawberry Filling

1 cup all-purpose flour

⅔ cup milk

2 egg whites

1 egg

3 tablespoons sugar

3 tablespoons unsweetened cocoa powder

1 tablespoon butter, melted and cooled

½ teaspoon salt

2 teaspoons canola oil

3 tablespoons strawberry fruit spread

3½ cups sliced fresh or thawed frozen strawberries

½ cup thawed frozen whipped topping

Fresh mint leaves (optional)

1. Combine flour, milk, egg whites, egg, sugar, cocoa, butter and salt in large bowl; whisk until smooth and well blended.

2. Brush medium Red Copper™ Pan with ¼ teaspoon oil; heat over medium heat. Pour about ¼ cup batter into center of pan. Immediately pick up pan and swirl to coat with batter. Cook 1 minute or until crêpe is dull on top and edges are dry. Turn and cook 30 seconds. Remove to plate and repeat with remaining oil and batter.

3. Stir strawberry fruit spread in medium bowl until softened. Add strawberries; toss to coat.

4. Spoon about ¼ cup strawberry mixture down center of each crêpe; roll up to enclose filling. Top each serving with 2 tablespoons whipped topping. Garnish with mint.

MAKES 8 CRÊPES (ABOUT 4 SERVINGS)

Apple Cranberry Crumble

- 4 large apples (about 1⅓ pounds), peeled and cut into ¼-inch slices
- 2 cups fresh or frozen cranberries
- ⅓ cup granulated sugar
- 6 tablespoons all-purpose flour, divided
- 1 teaspoon apple pie spice, divided
- ¼ teaspoon salt, divided
- ½ cup chopped walnuts
- ¼ cup old-fashioned oats
- 2 tablespoons packed brown sugar
- ¼ cup (½ stick) butter, cut into small pieces

1. Preheat oven to 375°F.

2. Combine apples, cranberries, granulated sugar, 2 tablespoons flour, ½ teaspoon apple pie spice and ⅛ teaspoon salt in large bowl; toss to coat. Spoon into medium Red Copper™ Pan.

3. Combine remaining 4 tablespoons flour, walnuts, oats, brown sugar, remaining ½ teaspoon apple pie spice and ⅛ teaspoon salt in medium bowl; mix well. Cut in butter with pastry blender or two knives until mixture resembles coarse crumbs. Sprinkle over fruit mixture in pan.

4. Bake 50 to 60 minutes or until filling is bubbly and topping is lightly browned.

MAKES 4 SERVINGS

Pineapple Orange Snack Cake

1 can (8 ounces) crushed pineapple in juice, undrained

1 cup orange juice, divided

2 tablespoons firmly packed dark brown sugar

1⅓ cups all-purpose flour

¼ cup granulated sugar

¼ cup powdered nonfat milk

2 teaspoons baking powder

½ teaspoon grated orange peel

3 egg whites

2 tablespoons canola oil

1 teaspoon vanilla

1. Preheat oven to 350°F.

2. Drain pineapple in fine mesh strainer, reserving liquid. Place large Red Copper™ Pan over high heat. Add pineapple juice and ½ cup orange juice. Bring to a boil; continue boiling 2½ minutes or until liquid measures ¼ cup. Remove pan from heat; add brown sugar to measured liquid in pan. Stir until blended. Using teaspoon, spoon pineapple evenly over brown-sugar mixture. *Do not stir.* Set aside.

3. Combine flour, granulated sugar, powdered milk, baking powder and orange peel in medium bowl; stir to blend. Add remaining ½ cup orange juice, egg whites, oil and vanilla. Using electric mixer, beat on low speed to blend. Increase to medium speed and beat 2 minutes or until smooth. Spoon batter evenly over pineapple mixture in pan.

4. Bake 30 to 35 minutes or until toothpick inserted in center comes out clean. Place on cooling rack 5 minutes. Loosen edges with knife and place plate over pan. Invert, scraping any remaining pineapple from pan and spooning on top of cake. Cut into eight wedges and serve warm.

MAKES 8 SERVINGS

Enlightened Apple Crisp

2 tablespoons granola with almonds

1 red apple (8 ounces), such as Gala, diced into ½-inch pieces

1 tablespoon dried sweetened cranberries

¼ teaspoon apple pie spice or ground cinnamon

1 teaspoon butter

2 teaspoons sugar

¼ teaspoon almond extract

1. Place granola in small resealable food storage bag. Crush lightly with rolling pin to form coarse crumbs; set aside.

2. Heat large Red Copper™ Pan over medium heat; spray with nonstick cooking spray. Add apple, cranberries and apple pie spice; cook and stir 4 minutes or until apples are just tender.

3. Remove from heat; stir in butter, sugar and almond extract. Spoon into two dessert bowls; sprinkle with granola. Serve immediately.

MAKES 2 SERVINGS

Note: You may prepare apple mixture up to 8 hours in advance; top with granola and ice cream at time of serving. To rewarm crisp, microwave apple mixture 20 to 30 seconds on HIGH or until warm before adding granola and ice cream.

Sweet 'n Easy Fruit Crisp Bowls

2 tablespoons granola with almonds

Nonstick cooking spray

1 red apple (8 ounces), such as Gala, diced into ½-inch pieces

1 tablespoon dried sweetened cranberries

¼ teaspoon apple pie spice or ground cinnamon

1 teaspoon butter

1 teaspoon sugar

¼ teaspoon almond extract

Vanilla ice cream

1. Place granola in small resealable food storage bag; crush lightly to form coarse crumbs. Set aside. Heat large Red Copper™ Pan over medium heat; coat with cooking spray. Add apples, cranberries and apple pie spice; cook 4 minutes or until apples are just tender, stirring frequently.

2. Remove from heat, stir in butter, sugar and almond extract. Spoon into two dessert bowls. Sprinkle with granola and spoon ice cream on top. Serve immediately.

MAKES 2 SERVINGS

Note: You may make the apple mixture up to 8 hours in advance and top with granola and ice cream at time of serving. To rewarm crisp, microwave apple mixture (before adding granola and ice cream) 20 to 30 seconds on HIGH or until slightly heated.

Cinnamon Tortilla with Cream Cheese & Strawberries

2 teaspoons sugar

⅛ teaspoon ground cinnamon

1 (6-inch) flour tortilla

Nonstick cooking spray

1 tablespoon cream cheese

⅓ cup fresh strawberry slices

1. Combine sugar and cinnamon in small bowl; mix well. Heat large Red Copper™ Pan over medium heat.

2. Lightly spray one side of tortilla with cooking spray; sprinkle with cinnamon mixture.

3. Place tortilla, cinnamon side down, in hot pan. Cook 2 minutes or until lightly browned. Remove from pan.

4. Spread uncooked side of tortilla with cream cheese; arrange strawberries down center of tortilla. Roll up tortilla to serve.

MAKES 1 SERVING

Cheesecake Swirl Brownies

1 package (about 18 ounces) brownie mix, plus ingredients to prepare mix

4 ounces cream cheese, softened

1 egg

3 tablespoons sugar

¼ teaspoon vanilla

⅓ cup semisweet chocoate chips

1. Preheat oven to 350°F. Prepare brownie mix according to package directions; spread in Red Copper™ Square Dance Pan.

2. Combine cream cheese, egg, sugar and vanilla in small bowl; stir to blend. Spoon cream cheese mixture by tablespoonfuls over brownie batter; cut through mixture with knife to make marble design. Sprinkle with chocolate chips.

3. Bake 40 to 45 minutes or until toothpick comes out clean. Cool slightly before cutting into squares.

MAKES 9 SERVINGS

Index

Strawberry Banana
French Toast (page 14)

METRIC CONVERSION CHART

VOLUME MEASUREMENTS (dry)

1/8 teaspoon = 0.5 mL
1/4 teaspoon = 1 mL
1/2 teaspoon = 2 mL
3/4 teaspoon = 4 mL
1 teaspoon = 5 mL
1 tablespoon = 15 mL
2 tablespoons = 30 mL
1/4 cup = 60 mL
1/3 cup = 75 mL
1/2 cup = 125 mL
2/3 cup = 150 mL
3/4 cup = 175 mL
1 cup = 250 mL
2 cups = 1 pint = 500 mL
3 cups = 750 mL
4 cups = 1 quart = 1 L

VOLUME MEASUREMENTS (fluid)

1 fluid ounce (2 tablespoons) = 30 mL
4 fluid ounces (1/2 cup) = 125 mL
8 fluid ounces (1 cup) = 250 mL
12 fluid ounces (1 1/2 cups) = 375 mL
16 fluid ounces (2 cups) = 500 mL

WEIGHTS (mass)

1/2 ounce = 15 g
1 ounce = 30 g
3 ounces = 90 g
4 ounces = 120 g
8 ounces = 225 g
10 ounces = 285 g
12 ounces = 360 g
16 ounces = 1 pound = 450 g

DIMENSIONS

1/16 inch = 2 mm
1/8 inch = 3 mm
1/4 inch = 6 mm
1/2 inch = 1.5 cm
3/4 inch = 2 cm
1 inch = 2.5 cm

OVEN TEMPERATURES

250°F = 120°C
275°F = 140°C
300°F = 150°C
325°F = 160°C
350°F = 180°C
375°F = 190°C
400°F = 200°C
425°F = 220°C
450°F = 230°C

BAKING PAN SIZES

Utensil	Size in Inches/Quarts	Metric Volume	Size in Centimeters
Baking or Cake Pan (square or rectangular)	8×8×2	2 L	20×20×5
	9×9×2	2.5 L	23×23×5
	12×8×2	3 L	30×20×5
	13×9×2	3.5 L	33×23×5
Loaf Pan	8×4×3	1.5 L	20×10×7
	9×5×3	2 L	23×13×7
Round Layer Cake Pan	8×1½	1.2 L	20×4
	9×1½	1.5 L	23×4
Pie Plate	8×1¼	750 mL	20×3
	9×1¼	1 L	23×3
Baking Dish or Casserole	1 quart	1 L	—
	1½ quart	1.5 L	—
	2 quart	2 L	—